£2-00

...re for Your Stick Insect

CONTENTS

Photos by:
**Nick Baker,
Paul Brock,
David Alderton,
Russell Willis**

©2002 by Kingdom Books PO9 5TT ENGLAND
Printed in China through Printworks Int. Ltd.

Far left: a female Giant Prickly Stick Insect (*Extatosoma tiaratum*). Middle: A male of the same variety.

Stick insects appeal to people of all ages. They can be accommodated without difficulty in a flat or house where keeping other pets such as dogs and cats would be impossible. Although stick insects do not become tame, their unusual shapes, colours and life styles offer a fascinating insight into the natural world. It is also probable that they will breed, providing you with a further source of interest.

Whereas some insects, such as flies, rely on their speed of movement to escape predators, stick insects use a combination of camouflage and immobility to avoid detection. Many species do look like small twigs, blending in against a branch.

Stick insects belong to a group of insects called phasmids. This description comes from the Latin word phasma, meaning 'ghost', and refers to the fact that they are hard to see. Many stick insects are shades of green and brown, and they can alter their coloration to some extent to blend into their background.

Some species, such as the Javanese (*Orxines macklotti*) have evolved further protection by growing what appear to be areas of moss on their bodies. This provides so-called disruptive camouflage, breaking up the outline of the insect's body and helping to disguise its presence still further.

Zoologists have identified over 2500 different species of stick insect and there are many others still awaiting discovery. They can grow up to 33cm (13in) long and most species tend to have a narrow, elongated body shape, although there are exceptions, such as the Jungle Nymph (*Heteropteryx dilatata*), which has a relatively broad body.

Many stick insects live in trees, so it is not surprising that a number of species have evolved the ability to fly. The wings, when present, are usually kept folded over the back. They are not generally ready fliers but, if disturbed, they take flight to escape the clutches of a predator. Those species without wings simply drop to the ground, remaining inert for several minutes until the danger has passed, and then climb back up again.

Parts Of The Stick Insect

The stick insect's body is divided into various segments, consisting of three basic parts. The head, complete with mouth parts on the underside, attaches to the middle part of the body, known as the thorax. Thin projections, called antennae, are also present on the head. These help the stick insect to find its way around. There is also a pair of compound eyes, resembling large dots, visible on the stick insect's head. These allow it to detect movement easily.

The thorax is divided into three segments. The first pair of legs attach to the relatively short front portion, called the prothorax. The longer mesothoracic segment anchors the second pair of legs, while the third pair attach at the rear of the metathorax.

The legs themselves are also segmented and are very important for the stick insect's well-being. Loss of legs, which may occur through overcrowding, can make it difficult for the stick insect to move around and obtain food. The legs end in small sharp claws, enabling the insect to maintain its grip and walk along a branch without difficulty.

The thorax also provides the point of attachment for the wings, if these are present. They are kept folded with their outer surfaces disguised to blend in with the stick insect's general appearance

The final section of the body is the abdomen, and is relatively long. In many cases the sides of the stick insect's body are both disguised and protected with spines and, in some cases, these may extend down on to the legs. Although the legs themselves are usually quite slender, they expand in some species to provide additional camouflage.

Obtaining Stick Insects

A pet shop in your area might stock stick insects or be able to obtain them for you. Alternatively, you may have to track down a specialist entomological supplier, who can supply you with either eggs or live stick insects. It is possible to have these dispatched in special packaging by mail if you cannot find a source near to where you live.

Joining the Phasmid Study Group offers the best way of locating fellow enthusiasts in your area. Members of this group usually breed both the common and some of the rarer stick insects. They are likely to have surplus stock available from time to time which will be advertised in the group's publications.

Eurycantha calcarata or Giant Spiny Stick Insect: the female can grow up to 15cm (6in), but the males are shorter, as is often the case with stick insects.

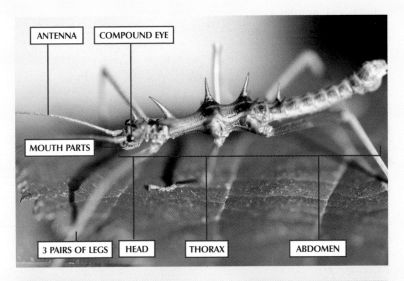

ANTENNA

COMPOUND EYE

MOUTH PARTS

3 PAIRS OF LEGS

HEAD

THORAX

ABDOMEN

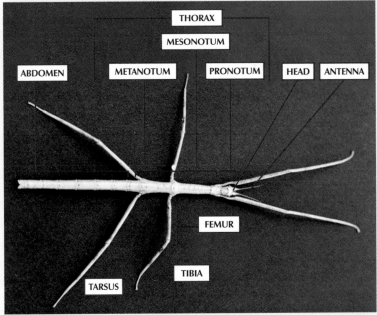

THORAX

MESONOTUM

ABDOMEN

METANOTUM

PRONOTUM

HEAD

ANTENNA

FEMUR

TIBIA

TARSUS

SELECTION

All the commonly-available stick insects can generally be maintained on a similar diet, ensuring that their care is straightforward. When handling stick insects, always take care to restrain them by the sides of the body, watching out for any sharp spines or projections which could be painful to touch. If necessary, you can wear a thin glove, but never hold the insect tightly, as this could injure it. Stick insects often grip strongly on to branches in their quarters, so you may have to prise their legs carefully away from the perch before lifting them.

Indian or Laboratory Stick Insect (*Carausius morosus*)

This is undoubtedly the best known of all stick insects among enthusiasts, and was also probably the first stick insect to be kept. In the early 1900s it was used for physiological experiments, which is why it became known as the Laboratory Stick Insect.

This species has a cylindrical body shape and tends to be a relatively dark shade of yellowish-green. There is a bright red area visible at the top of its front legs. It grows to about 10cm (4in) when adult.

Male Indian Stick Insects are very rare and, in any case, do not appear to mate, with females reproducing parthenogenetically (see page 28). The male is slightly smaller in size with a reddish underside to its thorax.

These stick insects can usually be kept quite satisfactorily at room temperature without extra heat, although this may be needed if there is no heat source in the room during cold weather. Feeding is straightforward, as they eat either bramble or privet.

Mature females lay relatively small numbers of eggs over a fairly lengthy period of time, eventually adding up to several hundred. Their eggs are dark brown in colour and look very much like seeds. Hatching takes about four months and the young nymphs, which resemble miniature adults, will moult for the last time when they are about five months old. They can live for up to a year.

Giant Prickly Stick Insect or Macleay's Spectre (*Extatosoma tiaratum*)

This is one of the most impressive species, which originate from Queensland and New South Wales in Australia. Today's captive strains are mainly descended from stock obtained from Queensland during the 1960s.

Female Giant Prickly Stick Insects can average 12cm (5in) and may grow to a size of 20cm (8in) or more if their legs are included. Although they possess rudimentary wings, these are not functional. Males, by contrast, can be recognised easily; they are smaller, averaging around 15cm (6in) and they can fly. These stick insects should be maintained at a

The common Indian (Laboratory) Stick Insect.

temperature of about 24°C (75°F) and can be fed on bramble, although they do eat oak, eucalpyptus and rose leaves when these are available.

Adults need to be handled carefully because they can inflict painful pricks with their sharp spines. It is essential to have stout branches in their quarters to support the weight of the females. Their eggs are greyish with buff streaking, with a swelling evident at one end. Keep these in a reasonably humid environment and at a similar temperature to the adults; otherwise hatchability is likely to be poor. Patience is also needed because these stick insects can take 6–10 months to hatch.

A newly-hatched Giant Prickly Stick Insect.

The nymphs measure about 1.25cm (0.5in) when they emerge from their eggs and are a dark shade of reddish-black at this stage. The lid to their quarters needs to be secure as they climb readily. The nymphs undergo a series of moults over the next five months.

Before making the first moult, they turn sandy-brown in colour and, as they grow larger, they can usually be sexed without difficulty. Females are brighter in colour and slightly larger, with soft spikes visible on their abdomen. Regular spraying will be beneficial. If conditions are not too dry, they may become dark in appearance. Giant Prickly Stick Insects do sometimes reproduce parthenogenetically, but normally they mate once they have moulted for the last time

Pink-winged Stick Insect or Madagascan Stick Insect (*Sipyloidea sipylus*)

A lively and active species with a large distribution in the wild, the Pink-winged Stick Insect ranges from parts of Asia and Madagascar, off the east coast of Africa where the culture stock originates from. The delicate wings of this species are pinkish with the remainder of the body being a light shade of brown. Remove any large thorns on brambles or roses used as food or the wings could be damaged.

The Pink-winged Stick Insect is parthenogenetic in its reproductive habits, and is similar in size to the Indian species. Again, males are sometimes bred and they can be distinguished by their smaller size. Once they are mature, females lay eggs but, unlike most species which scatter their eggs, these use a special gum to stick their eggs to the food plant, so do not discard branches of bramble without checking. When cleaning out their quarters, take care to ensure that none of the mature insects fly off. If they twitch their middle pair of legs, this is a sign that flight is likely.

A few hundred eggs are laid and hatching is rapid, usually about six weeks to four months later. At first, the young are green, which helps them to blend in against the food plant. They may be slow to eat, but keeping them with older individuals should encourage them to start browsing. Try to avoid moving the young nymphs because they are frail at this stage.

Giant Spiny Stick Insect (*Eurycantha calcarata*)
Not to be confused with the Giant Prickly Stick Insect (*Extatosoma tiaratum*), the distribution of this species is centred on New Guinea and various nearby islands, including New Britain. Females grow to about 15cm (6in) in size and have a pointed tip to the abdomen, whereas males are about 2.5cm (1in) shorter, with a broad end. One of the spikes on the femur at the top of each of the male's hind legs is also much larger than those of females.

Giant Spiny Stick Insects are unusual in that they live mostly on the ground rather than climbing trees. They need a different type of accommodation with hiding places such as pieces of cork bark on the floor of their quarters where they can retreat. These stick insects feed on a range of vegetation and may even eat grass. However, bramble and oak are the most suitable food plants.

The female Giant Spiny Stick Insect buries her eggs in a suitable container. The eggs have a brownish, marbled appearance, and can be kept in damp vermiculite (as sold for plants). It is important that they do not dry out, as fewer will hatch successfully.

Hatching may take place at any time from about three to six months after egg-laying or even longer. The young are brown when they emerge from their eggs but become mottled in colour after their first moult. These stick insects need to be handled carefully because of their sharp leg spines. They may also give off an unpleasant odour if threatened.

It is a good idea to separate males as they mature, since they can be aggressive to each other. A shallow dish of water for drinking purposes and to maintain the relative humidity in their quarters is useful, or leaves may be sprayed regularly. Giant Spiny Stick Insects can be long-lived with a life expectancy of nearly two years from hatching.

Jungle Nymph (*Heteropteryx dilatata*)

This truly spectacular stick insect originates from the jungles of Malaysia, and is also found in Sumatra, Java, Sarawak and Thailand. It is very easy to tell the sexes apart. Males are significantly smaller and brown in colour, with attractive wings that allow them to fly, while adult females are a beautiful shade of lime green, attaining a length of nearly 18cm (7in). Occasionally, yellow forms are reared. They have two pairs of rudimentary wings which resemble small leaves and are covered in small, sharp spines, especially on their legs. Should your finger slip when holding one of these stick insects, it is likely to clamp its leg, digging the spikes into your finger.

Relatively spacious and warm quarters, heated to about 24°C (75°F), suit these stick insects well. Regular spraying helps to replicate the relative humidity in their jungle home. Secure branches for climbing purposes must be incorporated into their accommodation. Jungle Nymphs feed well on bramble and are essentially arboreal by nature.

A large, female Jungle Nymph (*Heteropteryx dilatata*).

An adult female Jungle Nymph.

A male Costa Rican Stick Insect (*Calynda brocki*) .

The female will only descend to the ground under cover of darkness to lay her eggs. These are laid into a soft area of the substrate by means of the egg-laying tube (ovipositor), at the end of her abdomen. A small container of damp peat can be provided for this purpose with its acidic nature helping to combat the growth of any moulds.

The eggs are quite delicate and need to be kept moist so that they do not dessicate (dry out) during the incubation period, which can last for up to 17 months. They should also be kept warm and not disturbed although, in spite of every care, often hatchability is low. The young will grow reasonably slowly and the female can soon be recognised by the presence of her ovipositor. It may take up to 18 months before they are mature and they may live for a further 12 months or so.

Other Stick Insects

Asiatic species tend to be most commonly kept and among those which you may encounter is the Annam (*Baculum extradentatum*), with today's stock having originated from Vietnam during the 1950s. It is an attractive shade of reddish-brown, and quite slender in appearance. Females, growing to about 10cm (4in) long, are significantly larger than males. Increasingly, captive strains of this species appear to be becoming parthenogenetic.

The Thai Stick Insect (*Baculum thaii*) has a similar shape, resembling a twig in appearance. It first became available during the 1970s and has proved to be prolific. The sexes can be distinguished easily with males being slimmer and having white eyes. Females tend to be green in colour rather than brown, but this is not an entirely reliable method of distinguishing between the sexes.

A large, bulky species from Australia which is well established in collections is the Queensland Titan (*Acrophylla wuelfingi*). Females of this species can grow to 18cm (7in) long roughly, with males being smaller. Both sexes have wings, but only the darker males can fly. Care is similar to that recommended for the Giant Prickly Stick Insect but slightly lower relative humidity is preferable. Their dark eggs are relatively small and they

A female Costa Rican Stick Insect.

collections. The Costa Rican Stick Insect (*Calynda brocki*) is a particularly striking phasmid from this part of the world. Large females can reach 18cm (7in) long and are usually green or brown in colour, sometimes with

A species related to the stick insect is the Leaf-insect. This is a female *Phyllium bioculatum*, common in the Seychelles.

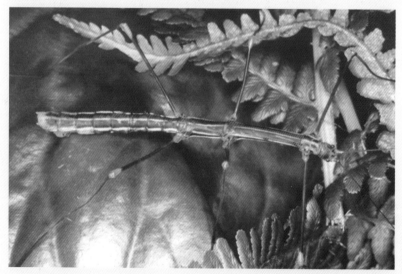

A Peruvian Fern (*Oreophoetes peruana*). This is a gynandromorph; in other words, it is part male, part female. This has a female body shape but typical male colouration.

can take 6–12 months to hatch, with the nymphs being surprisingly large, measuring up to 2.5cm (1in) long.

North American walking sticks are not commonly kept, partly because they are not especially striking in appearance, but others from parts of Central and South America have become quite well established in

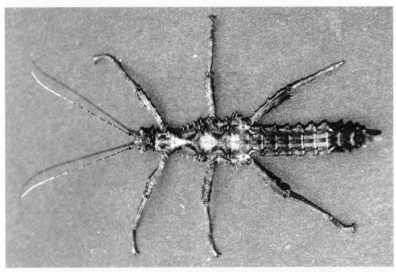

A female Borneo Thorney (*Aretaon asperrimus*); note the visible ovipositor.

A female Annam Stick Insect (*Baculum extradentatum*).

a pair of prominent white stripes running down the upper surface of their body. Males in contrast are smaller and have claspers on the top of their abdomen which they use during mating.

One of the most popular Caribbean species is the Trinidad Log Stick Insect (*Creoxylus spinosus*) , which is a chunky phasmid, looking rather like a miniature log and growing to about 7.5cm (3in) overall. It is brownish in colour and males can be distinguished by their wings. As well as bramble, these stick insects will also eat ivy.

If you purchase any of the more unusual stick insects, it is worth enquiring about their food preferences. For example, a very attractive South American species, called the Peruvian Fern Stick Insect (*Oreophoetes peruana*), requires fern fronds, such as those of the Boston Fern, as its food source. African stick insects have proved much harder to persuade to take substitute food plants and so are rare in collections. They naturally tend to favour acacia and no ready alternative has yet been found for this plant.

Equipment

Accommodation for stick insects does not need to be elaborate, although there are relatively expensive set-ups available from some entomological suppliers. One of the most important factors to bear in mind is that the quarters must be sufficiently tall to allow the insects to hang down vertically when they are moulting. They can then wriggle out of their old skin without difficulty. As a guide, therefore, be sure that the height of the accommodation is twice the maximum length of the stick insects which you are keeping.

The other aspects of housing which is obviously important is not to overcrowd the stick insects. Overcrowding can result in the insects chewing each others' legs and, especially if more than one leg is affected, arboreal species then have difficulty in climbing and feeding.

Your pet shop is likely to be able to supply everything that you need to house your stick insects. One of the best housing options is a plastic container with a removable ventilated roof section, which is sold in various colours. This is produced in a range of sizes, making it ideal for stick insects of all kinds, and is relatively inexpensive compared with other forms of housing such as aquaria.

You do need to take care, however, because some nymphs may slip out through the ventilation slits in the top of the unit. Placing strips of masking tape over the lid to reduce the size of the air spaces (which will not harm the stick insects) should be enough to prevent them escaping.

Heating can be arranged quite easily, using a slender flexible heating mat. These too are available in a range of sizes, being produced for vivaria, and are only 1mm thick. They can be positioned either under the stick insects' quarters or attached to one of the sides.

The heat output of these pads can be controlled by a thermostat, while the internal temperature can be monitored by a digital thermometer, as sold for aquaria. This simply needs to be stuck

A plastic container with a removable ventilated roof section. Stick insects should be able to hang upside down to moult.

on the front of the accommodation. The cost of running this type of heating is very low and it may not always be necessary to invest in a thermostat, depending on the wattage of the mat concerned, particularly if only one half of the unit is heated.

If you prefer, you can buy a vivarium as sold for reptiles and amphibians which will already have this equipment in place, although it will be relatively expensive compared with the plastic tank and hood. However, there may be less risk of young stick insects escaping, depending on the type of ventilation provided in the vivarium. As it is constructed of melamine, this type of unit is also heavier.

The third option is to use an aquarium with a suitable hood of the type used for converting aquaria into suitable housing for reptiles and amphibians. A glass tank of the type favoured today, with panels stuck together with silicone sealant, can be used to house a large number of stick insects if it is big enough. Unfortunately, such tanks are also heavy and easily broken, so they should not be moved more than is necessary.

Stick insects are not especially messy, so that a paper lining on the floor which extends up the sides of their quarters should catch most of their droppings, without the need to lift the tank regularly for cleaning purposes. If necessary, with the stick insects safely out of the way, the inside of the tank could be vacuumed using a suitable attachment to remove any droppings which have accumulated on the floor, which saves having to move the tank at all.

Another housing possibility, although one which is harder to clean, is a black cylindrical net enclosure of the type used to house butterflies. These are sold by entomological suppliers and can be stored flat when not in use. The stick insects can climb easily on the mesh whereas in traditional accommodation they usually spend most of their time attached to the food plants. There are drawbacks with these nets, however, including the fact that they are difficult to heat unless a light bulb is used. This is not really a satisfactory option and also there is less control over humidity than when the stick insects are housed in a more conventional set-up.

A better option is to purchase the black nylon netting separately. This can then be cut and fixed to the sides of a glass tank, allowing the stick insects to use much more of the area available to them.

Another alternative is to use the netting to build a more traditional enclosure based on a wooden framework. You can use 1.25cm or 2.5cm (0.5in or 1in) timber for the framework, building the cage to a sectional design. Carefully glue the lengths together and allow them to dry before assembly, or you can screw them together. Cut the mesh neatly and fold it around the sides, ensuring there are no gaps through which the stick

The old skin of a Spiny Devil (*Eurycantha calcarata*).

insects can escape. The rear panel can be made of thin melamine as should the base, allowing a flexible heating pad to be fitted if needed. This type of heater is usually still effective through a covering up to 1.25cm (0.5in) thick.

The major advantage of this type of unit is that it should provide escape-proof quarters, even for newly-hatched stick insects, and can be constructed to almost any size. In addition, it can be designed for ease of cleaning if the base segment is made so that it detaches from the rest of the unit.

You do need to take care to ensure that the nylon mesh is positioned so that it is taut

If black net is attached to the sides of a glass container, the stick insects can climb up it.

on the frames, using a staple gun to anchor it in place. Hinging the top of the unit in place will allow you to feed the stick insects without difficulty.

Temporary Accommodation

When moving stick insects, especially young nymphs, it is important to have secure, escape-proof accommodation available. A variety of glass or plastic containers, complete with a piece of bramble or similar plant, can be recommended for this purpose. Small holes can be punched in the lid first for ventilation.

The most important thing to remember when transporting stick insects is never to leave them in direct sunlight, for example on the back seat of a car. Even though they come from tropical areas, the temperature can soon rise to a lethal limit, especially in a car parked in hot sun. Keep the container under one of the seats, or somewhere in the shade.

Floor coverings

The droppings of stick insects are relatively dry and it is not essential to clean their quarters every day. It helps to use a floor covering that catches the droppings effectively so that they can be removed without difficulty.

Sheets of newspaper, although not especially attractive, can be used for this purpose and make a cheap and easily disposable lining.

A better option, particularly with mature stick insects which randomly scatter their eggs, may be to use sheets of plain white paper. Apart from being more attractive, this should also help you to spot any eggs among the droppings, whereas they will be harder to pick out against newspaper.

To make cleaning easier, you can construct a lining tray quite easily out of cardboard. This should have slightly raised edges, so that you can lift out the tray and the paper together. If you simply fold up the sheets of paper to remove them from the accommodation, eggs and droppings become

A Guadeloupe Stick Insect (*Lamponius guerini*).

A Peruvian Fern Stick Insect (female).

mixed, making the removal of the eggs a more unpleasant task. A small paintbrush is helpful for this purpose, allowing you to roll the eggs out easily.

It is not a good idea to leave the eggs undisturbed in the droppings of the adult stick insects, as they are likely to turn mouldy. Young nymphs hatching into this type of environment are at greater risk of succumbing to fungal infections as a result.

FEEDING AND GENERAL CARE

Stick insects are not difficult to keep. Their needs are few, but they still require careful husbandry in order to thrive and have a good life.

Feeding

Although it is not possible to buy food for stick insects in pet shops, it is not too difficult to maintain a regular supply of greenstuff for them. As mentioned before, almost all the commonly-available species feed on bramble.

What you need is access to a supply of bramble (blackberry) leaves throughout the year. Although these grow readily in areas of woodland, this does not necessarily mean that you have to collect supplies every day. Indeed, you may well be able to grow sufficient supplies at home. This has a number of advantages, and means that you should always have a fresh supply available, especially if you cultivate bramble in pots or tubs sheltered from the worst of the winter weather. New shoots should continue to grow, especially if the plant is kept in a well-lit area.

During the cold, dark months, the plants do not grow fast outdoors

The stick insect has moulted and left its old case behind.

A young stick insect on a bramble plant.

The female Giant Spiny Stick Insect has a more pointed abdomen than the male.

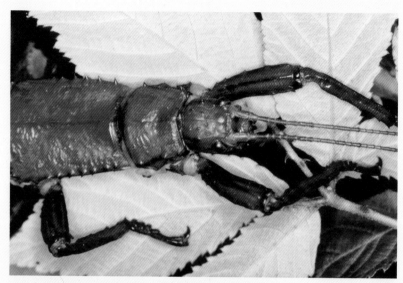

A Giant Spiny Stick Insect preparing to eat its meal.

Bramble – the staple food of a stick insect.

and will produce few, if any, new shoots. Those leaves which are accessible are likely to be old and rather tough, making them less desirable as a food source, especially for nymphs. Should you need to use any shoots in this condition, trim off any unappetising brown edges before offering them to the stick insects, which otherwise may be reluctant to eat properly.

Cultivating the bramble at home also means that you can be certain that it has not been sprayed with any herbicides or similar chemicals, which could prove toxic to stick insects. As a further precaution, if collecting bramble from the wild, only choose localities well away from the road, where the risk of spraying will be slight.

Bramble grows readily off underground shoots and it can be a very invasive plant. This is why it is better to cultivate it in pots, where its growth can be contained, rather than planting it in a garden. Start by digging in the soil around a shoot, and trace its root system. Using a sharp knife, cut through this root some distance away from the shoot. You can then bury the root at a suitable depth in a pot. Provided that it is kept in a slightly shaded locality and not allowed to dry out, new shoots should start to develop rapidly, especially during the spring and summer months.

Before offering the bramble to the stick insects, it is a good idea to wash it, especially if it has been gathered in the wild. This should help to remove any soiling by wild animals. Shake the leaves to dry them off, and check the undersides for any signs of spiders' nests, cutting off any leaves

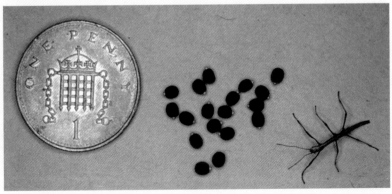

The eggs and newly-hatched young of an Indian (Laboratory) Stick Insect compared in size with a one penny piece.

which show signs of the characteristic whitish silk. These leaves are often slightly curled at their edges. Young spiders hatching in the stick insects' quarters may start to prey on their hosts, with small nymphs being at greatest risk.

It is better to supply the stick insects with entire shoots, complete with leaves attached. The stick insects can climb more easily around their quarters when provided with a whole food plant, rather than just leaves. In addition, the plant will provide them with greater height, particularly if placed within a suitable container.

The useful lifespan of the bramble as a food is prolonged if it is kept in water, but you must prevent the stick insects from gaining access to the water container or they may drown. Choose a narrow-necked vessel and stuff the sides with foil as a further precaution. Check also that the container is stable, especially in an enclosure housing the larger stick insects such as Jungle Nymphs.

If bramble is in short supply, particularly during the winter months, other plants you could offer include pyracantha, evergreen oak and rose leaves.

Should you have access to a natural food plant, such as eucalyptus, favoured by various Australian species, then you should offer this as you

A Vietnam Prickly Stick Insect.

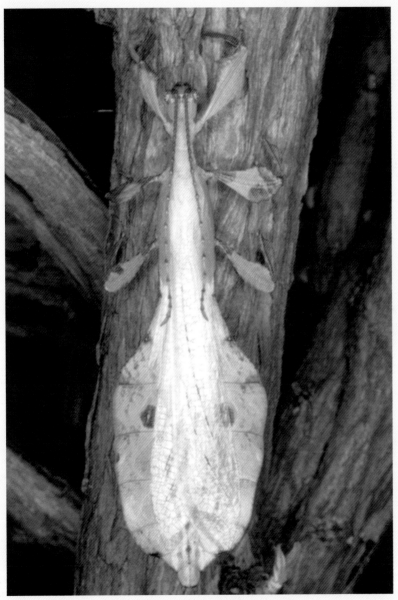

Male Leaf-insect from Java.

may obtain better results. Certain types of eucalyptus can be grown successfully in milder areas of the United Kingdom. It is better to make any changes to the diet after the stick insects have moulted, because their appetites are likely to be greater at this stage and they are more likely to accept unfamiliar foods.

Food should be constantly available to stick insects. Change the food plants once they start to wilt, taking care (especially with the smaller stick insects) that none remain on the discarded leaves. Water can be supplied for most species by means of a light misting with tepid water in the morning, although you should provide the *Eurycantha* species with a shallow dish of water for drinking purposes. Nymphs of this species can drown in their water container, so clean piece of tinfoil filled with a little water is a safer option than a small pot.

The enclosure also needs to be cleaned regularly, at least once a week. This is usually just a matter of changing the floor covering, although if a number of nymphs are being reared together, be sure that none slip out while your attention is directed elsewhere.

Health concerns

Stick insects are generally very healthy. Widespread deaths in a group are generally due to poor environmental conditions, which can include chilling, although dehydration is probably a more common cause of losses.

Problems are most likely to arise during the moulting period, during which most stick insects suspend themselves from a convenient branch or other attachment in their quarters, before splitting their skin in the vicinity of the thorax and wiggling out. You may notice that the stick insect loses its appetite prior to a moult. This is quite normal. After moulting, it remains largely inert for a few hours until its new skin has hardened. Moulting in this fashion is the only way in which a stick insect can grow. They are especially delicate at this stage, and should not be handled.

Stick insects generally live between six months and a year likely to be insecticides, such as fly killers, or flea sprays used on other domestic pets. Try to avoid using such chemicals in the home, because they can be wafted on air currents very easily so that toxic doses reach your pets before you are aware of the potential danger.

The eggs of stick insects are called ova. It is considerably cheaper to buy eggs rather than adult specimens, and you can have the enjoyment of watching the resulting nymphs grow up, ensuring that the stick insects live for as long as possible. You need to be patient until the nymphs start to hatch which could take several months. Try to find out when the eggs were laid, so that you can estimate when hatching is likely to occur. Adult stick insects have a much shorter lifespan than nymphs, because they are in the last phase of their life cycle.

Look carefully and you will see a white egg nestling in the ovipositor at the end of the abdomen.

From top to bottom: eggs of the Giant Spiny Stick Insect (*Eurycantha*), Indian or Laboratory Stick Insect (*Carausius morosus*), and Giant Prickly Stick Insect (*Extatosoma tiaratum*).

In a number of species, female stick insects can produce fertile ova without mating. This is called parthenogenesis. Having just one individual should result in the production of fertile eggs which hatch into females only. Where mating is necessary, however, it is generally quite easy to distinguish between the sexes, even before they are adult, so that recognising pairs is not difficult. Females are normally much larger than males and frequently have a egg-laying tube, or *ovipositor*, at the end of the abdomen.

It may be better to keep a male with two or three females if you are seriously interested in breeding your stick insects. However, do bear in mind that they are likely to produce many hundreds of eggs. Although in the wild only a small fraction of the offspring would survive through to adulthood, you could soon find yourself overrun with young nymphs.

Only one mating may be necessary to allow a female stick insect to produce fertile eggs throughout her life. She will store the male's sperm in her body. Giant Prickly Stick Insects are among the most prolific species and may lay as many as 1000 eggs. These are laid quite forcibly so that they are distributed over a wide area. In the wild, this means that the likelihood increases that a greater number of nymphs will find suitable food plants within easy reach when they hatch.

Stick insects which scatter their eggs need no special facilities for breeding purposes, but in the case of those which bury their eggs, such as the Giant Spiny, then you should provide a suitable container filled with moist peat for egg-laying purposes. The Pink-winged is the only commonly-kept species which actually glues its eggs on to its food plant. Do not attempt to remove the eggs, as this will probably affect their hatching. The best thing to do is to leave them in place and cut round them carefully, keeping the ova on the pieces of leaf until they hatch.
In all cases, the eggs tend to resemble seeds, with a flattened lid at one end through which the nymph will hatch in due course. They should be kept under similar conditions to the adult stick insects, with supplementary heat being useful for some species.

The long, variable hatching period of the eggs means that you could possibly miss eggs hatching, particularly as the nymphs do not emerge at one time. Spread them out over the floor of a small, clear-topped plastic container so it is easier to inspect them every day, as the hatching date draws close.

A small plant propagator can be used for this purpose, and also serves as a nursery area for the young nymphs as they hatch, and until they are large enough to be transferred elsewhere. If you do need to move them, use a paintbrush for this purpose. Encourage the nymph to grip on to the brush without touching its body directly, although keeping your hand underneath it just in case it does decide to relinquish its grip.

The hatchability of eggs does vary widely. It is generally higher in the case of stick insects which reproduce by mating rather than parthenogenetically. Keep a watch on the ventilation through the incubation period, because any mould developing on the eggs is likely to harm the eggs and nymphs.

Once the nymphs have hatched, make sure they have food within easy reach, otherwise they may starve. Although a light misting is important, especially for tropical species, too much water will not only promote mould, but can also lead to small nymphs drowning in droplets.

Most species can be reared quite easily and grow quickly.

Most species can be reared quite easily and grow quickly. Be sure to transfer them to larger accommodation as necessary to prevent overcrowding. They can be moved to new homes at any stage, but it may be better to wait until you are certain that they are eating properly and growing well.